Curriculum Integration

Twenty Questions — With Answers

Greeting his pupils the master asked,
What would you learn from me?
And the reply came:
How shall we care for our bodies?
How shall we rear our children?
How shall we work together?
How shall we live with our fellow man?
How shall we play?
For what ends shall we live?
And the teacher pondered these words
and sorrow was in his heart,
for his own learning touched not these things.

— sometimes attributed to Angelo Patri

CURRICULUM INTEGRATION
Twenty Questions — With Answers

by
Gert Nesin
John Lounsbury

Georgia Middle School Association

Georgia Middle School Association
6595G Roswell Road, PMB 749
Atlanta, GA 30328
(404) 256-4005

The Georgia Middle School Association is proud to publish the first in a series of monographs written for middle level educators. It is especially fitting that the introductory monograph be co-authored by a well-known Georgia scholar and national leader in middle level education, John Lounsbury, and one of Georgia's young scholars fresh out of the classroom where she practiced what she preaches, Gert Nesin. Their collaboration results in a significant contribution to the growing literature on curriculum integration.

The authors provide very realistic and direct responses to twenty of the most frequently asked questions about curriculum integration. This format makes it a very functional resource for teachers and teams to utilize as they struggle to move toward an integrated curriculum.

The Georgia Middle School Association appreciates the willingness of the authors to prepare a publication that will assist practicing teachers as they plan instruction for young adolescents. Special thanks goes to Mary Mitchell for assisting in the preparation of GMSA's first monograph.

— Ronnie Sheppard, Series Editor

ISBN: 0-9675081-0-X
Copyright ©1999 by Georgia Middle School Association.
Linda Hopping, Executive Director

Contents

Preface

Even as new attacks on the middle school are being launched, accumulating research data and abundant examples of successful practice combine to make it clear that the middle school is not a passing fad. The middle school concept is built on the strongest foundation possible, the best that is known about learning and a full understanding of human growth and development. Yet at the same time it has to be acknowledged that the movement's advancement and success to date has been more organizational than instructional. Middle schools have gained an identity, but they still lack full acceptance and implementation. The first decade of the new millennium, however, is certain to see continuing efforts to truly reform curriculum and classroom practices by implementing the middle school concept.

In the 90s, extensive "curriculum conversations" began occurring, kicked off in large part by James Beane's book, *A Middle School Curriculum: From Rhetoric to Reality* (1990, 1993). His strong case for an integrated curriculum helped encourage a number of courageous teams and teachers to move beyond the planned correlation of two or three subjects that has come to characterize interdisciplinary instruction. The book also reminded educators that there is a long and honorable history of such curriculum reforms that should be revisited.

The authors are admittedly strong, even passionate, supporters of curriculum integration. Yet we are also realists who recognize that for hundreds and hundreds of teams, interdisciplinary planning and instruction is proving to be a most satisfactory means of teaching young adolescents. What teaming makes possible has not yet been fully exploited, many seem to say; but it is working, parents support it; and student achievement is improving. There are, also, too many middle level schools still operating without teaming or without adequate common planning time. In such situations, curriculum integration is difficult to achieve. Then, there are numbers of other teachers, excellent teachers, whose philosophies and perceptions of teaching simply do not match the concepts of curriculum integration.

Perhaps as great a barrier as any to the expansion of curriculum integration at this time, however, is the narrowly defined but widely heard cry for accountability as measured by standardized test scores. When a school's success is determined almost solely by such scores and both the prescribed curriculum and the tests are organized by subject areas, schools and teachers otherwise anxious to invigorate schooling are caught in a bind. What curriculum integration calls for flies in the face of the assumptions underlying the various state and national reform proposals and their mandates. This is a reality that cannot be wished away or ignored.

Yet there are teachers and teams willing to take risks — for kids' sake. We hope this monograph will provide the information and the encouragement that will lead some committed teachers who are secure in their situations to instigate curriculum integration. While it is not the only way or even the best way for many good teachers, when one becomes aware of the real and relevant learnings possible in curriculum integration, one cannot help but be excited about what could be achieved "if only..."

These questions raised by Beane (1995) help us visualize the potential.

> What would happen if young people experienced these kinds of curriculum arrangements across several years?

> Having experienced the richness of these curriculum experiences, what might be a next and more sophisticated set of questions or projects in which young people might be involved?

> What would happen if the majority of middle school teachers undertook this kind of curriculum work, if a new generation of young people thought more critically, accessed information more easily, expected democratic participation, cared more deeply for others, demanded action on questions of justice, expected school to be about something of great significance?

> What would happen to our high schools, to our workplaces, to our colleges, to our society? (p. xi)

Idealistic? Of course. But the work of a growing host of middle level educators in the last decade gives hope that curriculum integration may ultimately become common if not universal practice. Could those words of Victor Hugo, uttered in 1852, be prophetic? "An invasion of armies can be resisted, but not an idea whose time has come."

— GN
— JL

1 What is curriculum integration?

G iven the misuse of this term it is well to start by saying what it is not. It is not an advanced level of interdisciplinary or multidisciplinary planning and teaching; it is not an occasional problem-based unit. James Beane (1995), the leading contemporary advocate of curriculum integration describes it thusly:

> Curriculum integration is not simply an organizational de-
> vice requiring cosmetic changes or realignments in lesson
> plans across various subject areas. Rather, it is a way of think-
> ing about what schools are for, about the sources of cur-
> riculum, and about the uses of knowledge. Curriculum inte-
> gration begins with the idea that the sources of curriculum
> ought to be problems, issues, and concerns posed by life
> itself. (p. 616)

Beane (1997) further states:
> Curriculum integration is a curriculum design that is con-
> cerned with enhancing the possibilities for personal and social
> integration through the organization of curriculum around
> significant problems and issues, collaboratively identified by
> educators and young people, without regard for subject-
> area boundaries. (pp. x-xi).

There are, then, four essential characteristics of curriculum integration:
1. **Students and teachers collaboratively plan the curriculum and how it is pursued.** The students do not tell the teacher what they want to study. The teacher is the leader and has responsibilities that go be-yond equal participation. As a professional educator, the teacher must assure that student decisions are thoroughly considered and lead to

1

educative experiences. But, on the other hand, collaboration does not mean the teacher manipulates students into agreeing with what he or she has determined beforehand. Both students and teachers may start with preconceived notions of what may happen, but neither uses authority to unilaterally turn those preconceptions into foregone plans and actions.

2. **Themes provide the organizing center for learning activities.** These themes are derived from student interests and concerns and must be socially significant. Therefore, a topic such as yo-yos would not be an acceptable theme in curriculum integration. Some educators believe that if students participate in determining themes, they will not approach the responsibility seriously. However, experience has shown that when students are asked about their concerns, they respond in a consistently profound way and construct themes of real significance. In a theme of *Power,* for example, students have asked such questions as "How reliable / truthful are the media?" "Will the United States ever not be a powerful country?" and "Will there ever be a president who isn't white, Christian, and male?"

3. **Learning takes place in a democratic classroom community.** Democracy in the classroom goes well beyond the simple idea of voting with the majority winning; here consensus replaces voting. Every person has the right to object to any decision and have that objection seriously considered. Plans must be adjusted until all decisions are acceptable to each individual. All members of the classroom community, teachers and students alike, truly have impact on decisions.

4. **Separate subjects no longer define the curriculum.** Personal concerns of social significance become the main focus of learning and the activities that facilitate learning. Curriculum mandates and traditional subject matter can and will be included but not in a pre-planned scope and sequence. Information and ideas relevant to the theme are ferreted out from any and all areas of knowledge.

Curriculum integration is not a new fad developed in the 1990s. Its foundations were laid by John Dewey (1938, 1956), who began at the turn of the 20th century to write about the importance of balancing the three curricular sources of school subjects, the needs of learners developmentally and individually, and the demands of citizens in a democratic society. He emphasized that learning should be focused on societal problems that have real meaning for young people and that subject matter should help them understand and solve those problems. Learning would then have immediate importance to students and would also prepare them for solving problems as participating citizens.

In the 1930s, educators, mainly at the junior high school level, began exploring curriculum integration, usually in the form of the core curriculum, a problem-centered block of time under the direction of one teacher. Although the core curriculum never disappeared, World War II, the Cold War, and the launching of Sputnik were among factors that curtailed its practice.

James A. Beane, who had participated in a core program as a high school student, became a leader in reviving the principles of the core curriculum in the 1990s. His seminal book, *A Middle School Curriculum, From Rhetoric to Reality* (1993), caught the attention of many educators, especially those involved in the middle school movement. Although he advocates the idea of curriculum integration, he never claims it as his own. Rather he readily acknowledges and recognizes the rich history of curriculum integration and the importance of its historical roots. Beane's effective speaking and writing continues to further the concept and encourages a number of teachers and teams to implement it.

When visiting a classroom where curriculum integration is being practiced, the routines may look very much like those in any other effectively operated classroom. Students may, for example, work by themselves, participate in small groups, or listen to a presentation by the teacher. Students may be involved in projects, even take a test. The teacher might move from individual to individual or group to group offering assistance as requested. What may not be clear from such an observation, however, becomes apparent when you talk to the students and discover their commitment to learning, concern for others, and the sense of ownership they possess. Talk to the teacher and discover a refreshing excitement about the students and teaching itself. Relationships are based on mutual respect, and the program of study has meaning for young people. All members of the classroom are part of an active learning community.

Curriculum integration is an approach to education that fosters active learning in a democratic environment. In many respects it is a reflection of one's belief about kids and learning. It is not a strategy to be followed in cookbook fashion but is a curriculum design that brings vitality and true relevance to the teaching / learning process. ⌘

2 What is the difference between interdisciplinary instruction and curriculum integration?

As already indicated, there is confusion over various terms related to curriculum organization. That confusion is well founded, for in the literature the terms are used in various ways to refer to diverse practices. There are, however, clear and substantial differences between curriculum integration and interdisciplinary instruction.

Interdisciplinary instruction, even though featuring the positive aspect of planned correlation, remains essentially separate subject. The theme, often more of a topic or a particular part of a subject area, is usually determined by the teachers. Then each teacher decides what his or her particular content area can contribute to the theme. For instance, when a team plans a unit on colonial times, students in math might investigate population growth and death rate; in social studies they examine the historical context; in science the growth of crops and the use of trees occupy them; while in language arts they read and respond to a historical novel based on colonial times. The unit might occasionally include some contributions from the unified arts or humanities; but whatever subject areas are included in a given unit, those areas remain relatively distinct and students know which class they are attending at a particular time. Figure 1 depicts such a unit.

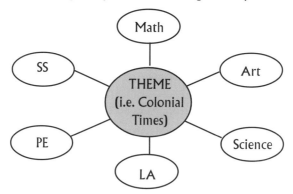

Figure 1 : Interdisciplinary Curriculum

The center of curriculum integration is a theme, but instead of learning about aspects of the theme from separate subject classes, students and teachers develop activities that explore the theme and the group's questions without reference to subject areas as such (Fig. 2). For instance, within the theme, *The Future,* students may look into their family history to make predictions about their future, investigate developing technology, research Nostradamus and psychics, and collect others' predictions of the future. Activities involve subject matter from various content areas as people investigate and solve problems, but they are not the source for those investigations. Students don't "do" math, followed by science, language arts, and social studies, but rather they engage in activities that involve these subjects and other fields of knowledge.

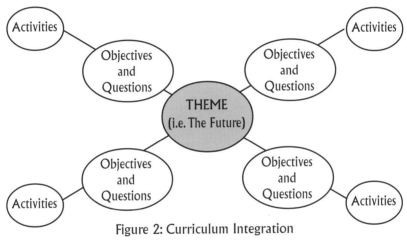

Figure 2: Curriculum Integration

The selection of themes is another point of departure between interdisciplinary instruction and curriculum integration. In interdisciplinary instruction, teachers generally decide the topic and theme based on the curriculum they are expected to cover. Social studies teachers may choose a theme such as World War I, while science teachers may center a unit on a topic such as weather. In contrast, in curriculum integration, the process of selecting a theme evolves from students' personal and social concerns. Therefore, themes tend to be larger and focus on a concept such as *change* or *cooperation and conflict.* Such themes have many possible directions and implications. After a theme is selected, students and teachers, in collaboration, determine what information will help them answer the questions identified and what activities may yield the needed understandings. Curriculum integration focuses first on genuine student concerns to build themes and then draws on elements of the required curriculum as well as other material in learning about these themes. Interdisciplinary instruction, on the other hand, chooses themes based on mandated curriculum and then considers how best to teach them to students.

The responsibilities of teachers and students vary considerably in the two approaches. (See Questions 10 and 11). Interdisciplinary curriculum is usually planned by teachers during common planning time or outside of school hours, apart from students, while planning in curriculum integration is done with students and is seen as an important part of the learning process. Themes selected reflect student concerns, and they help determine what activities and experiences will help them learn about the theme. Teachers take primary and often exclusive responsibility for assessment in interdisciplinary instruction. In curriculum integration, however, students help determine the standards for assessing their work and take major responsibility for their learning.

In summary, to determine whether a particular set of learning experiences should be labeled interdisciplinary curriculum or curriculum integration, it is best to examine the underlying assumptions of each plan. How were themes constructed and what is the center of those themes? How were students' needs considered in constructing and executing the themes? Was the subject matter predetermined or was it introduced because it contributed to understanding the theme and its many aspects? How and to what extent were students included in planning, monitoring, and assessing their own learning? These are some of the questions that get at the differences between true curriculum integration and interdisciplinary instruction. ⌘

All studies arise from aspects of the one earth and the one life lived upon it. We do not have a series of stratified earths, one of which is mathematical, another physical, another historical, and so on. We should not be able to live very long in any one taken by itself. We live in a world where all sides are bound together. All studies grow out of relations in the one great common world. When the child lives in varied but concrete and active relationship to this common world, his studies are naturally unified. It will not longer be a problem to correlate studies. The teacher will not have to resort to all sorts of devices to weave a little arithmetic into the history lesson, and the like.

— John Dewey, *School and Society*, 1900

3 Why should I implement curriculum integration?

F irst and foremost the answer is to improve student learning and increase student achievement. Curriculum integration is not being advocated because it is easier on teachers, less costly, or more "efficient." It is, in many respects more difficult, complex and demanding, but in operation it puts into practice the best that is known about learning and meets more adequately the needs of young adolescents in this critical stage of life. The traditional curriculum with its accompanying well-accepted instructional practices, it has to be realized, conflicts with the best ways to learn and develop intellectually while failing to offer support in many aspects of student development. To maximize student learning and growth it is necessary to break away from the basic subject areas and the accompanying overuse of passive learning. Curriculum integration transcends many of the barriers imposed by periods and subjects and engages students actively in meaningful learning activities. Higher test scores will ultimately be the result because learning has been improved.

The goals of middle level education are necessarily broad and numerous. The generally accepted goal of acquiring basic content and fundamental knowledge is certainly a continuing responsibility. So too is the mastering of basic skills even as the nature and extent of these skills to be mastered increases significantly. But the middle level institution, because it is responsible for youth during a major period of growth, has the responsibility of assisting youth in a number of social and personal needs, ones that cannot be ignored if real, lasting achievement is our goal. The difficulty of meeting these developmental tasks under the traditional curriculum has been widely recognized. Experience has demonstrated that teachers, instructing youth one after the other in the basic subjects, seldom have adequate opportunity to help students develop social relationships or understand the changes that puberty foists upon young adolescents, two priority concerns of all 10-14 year olds.

Curriculum integration, on the other hand, meets more fully all of these basic middle level goals. While the acquisition of basic information may not occur in the preordained order of typical scope and sequence charts, there is no evidence that students learn any less of the content normally included. In fact, they will acquire more extensive knowledge. And because what they study grows out of their concerns and interests, the knowledge gained will be retained long after information learned passively in order to pass a test has dissipated. There is genuine rigor in an integrated curriculum, a rigor that surpasses that imposed by the traditional curriculum that relies on extrinsic motivators. And since student concerns and interests provide the starting point, the often-heard but seldom realized need for curriculum relevance is assured. Topics that are rarely a part of separate subject instruction now have a rightful place in the curriculum. And student ownership, a requisite for real quality, is achieved. Indeed, it is the full and active part that students play in an integrated curriculum that is the real key to its ability to increase student achievement and build positive attitudes toward the school experience.

Along with teaching basic knowledge and skills, American schools are also responsible for preparing students for the democratic society in which they live. For most middle school classrooms, this largely means teaching the structure and interaction of our government. Curriculum integration goes well beyond; it develops the skills necessary for effective participation in a democracy. Young adolescents have the opportunity to learn how to collaboratively solve problems while considering diverse points of view. They learn to find, evaluate, synthesize, and use a variety of information to better understand problems and take responsible action. We expect our students to leave school and make important decisions about the direction of their local and national communities. In curriculum integration, students actually experience democracy.

In short, curriculum integration warrants further implementation because it will fulfill more effectively the general education goals that are universally endorsed by educators, parents, and citizens generally. ⌘

4 How do I get started with kids?

B y the time students start middle school, their experiences have led them to reach many assumptions about the ways school is conducted and learning is achieved. These assumptions are shared by many teachers and most parents as well. Consider the following assumptions or "beliefs":

- Teachers possess the knowledge that students need to learn.
- Teachers decide about what to study because they have more experience in both life and education.
- The separate subject organization is the best and possibly the only way to really learn the required curriculum.
- Learning is arduous, tedious, repetitive, and sometimes painful work requiring lots of paperwork and memorization.
- What school teaches us will equip us for the future.

These are only some of the assumptions that are integral in students' typical school experience. But are the assumptions valid?

Curriculum integration challenges every assumption about the role of teachers, the role of students, how learning takes place, and the organization of the curriculum. To launch curriculum integration the teacher needs to help students extract and examine various assumptions. This examination should start at the beginning of the school year, but it will be an ongoing task as assumptions have been built up over a long time through many experiences. Students must continually be reassured that they are learning what they need to learn even though "schooling" looks and feels different. Much unlearning has to go on to help students overcome the conditioning that has occurred.

Constant and honest reflection is essential if students are to break free of these assumptions. When given the chance students can identify learning experiences that were meaningful to them. This simple prompt can begin the process: "Think about a time when you learned something that you enjoyed and the learning stayed with you. Describe that experience." The discussions that follow about the characteristics of effective learning situations can lead to the identification of guidelines that can direct current learning. Students will have started the process of reflection and begun to shape their own learning environment.

Determining classroom behavior policies provides another way to initiate student involvement. Students are accustomed to entering a classroom where already-determined rules are posted and consequences are explained. They are expected to follow these rules but may never understand the justification for them. If teachers want students to take responsibility for their learning and actions, developing classroom guidelines is a good place to start. Consider having students reflect on a question such as: "If you were the best student you could be, what would you do both in and out of class?" The ensuing dialogue can lead to consensus on some general guidelines that place the responsibility for both thought and actions with the student. Thus, students become responsible for creating an effective learning environment. We underestimate the abilities of young people. We protect them too long, keep them in a passive role and, though well intended, our conscientious control of all aspects of their classrooms denies them opportunities to think, participate, and to really learn.

Developing positive student-student and teacher-student relationships is essential for students' participation. Therefore, it is necessary to take time to develop those relationships. Team-building challenges and games can assist in establishing a collaborative and caring community. Students may collectively develop questions and then interview each other using these questions. Following the interviews, students introduce one another or create posters about each other to be posted in the classroom. Throughout these activities, teachers should participate as much as possible to provide a role model for taking risks as well as to become part of the learning community.

Reflecting on learning characteristics, collaboratively determining classroom guidelines, and building relationships takes time, a lot of time. Some may question the value of these activities when time to cover the curriculum is already short. The payoff, however, comes throughout the rest of the year as students take more responsibility for their behavior, their learning, and each other.

After the class has taken several steps toward establishing a learning environment, academic concerns can be addressed more effectively. At this point, teachers and students may or may not be ready to actually begin collaboratively planning their curriculum. For those who are not ready, some interim steps may be helpful. The class may start with a short unit that has been planned by the teachers but which incorporates some student choice. Teachers inform students that they will soon be making more decisions about their learning. Throughout the unit, the teachers take time to explain how and why they make certain decisions about curriculum, activities, and assessment. Students are thereby introduced to the process of learning before they are given the responsibility for helping to plan the curriculum.

Another strategy is to explore the meaning of democracy, not only as a form of government, but as a philosophy of dealing with others, a way of life. Such a unit might culminate in writing a classroom constitution. Other teachers start by spending a portion of each day experimenting with the processes of curriculum integration and use the remainder of school hours in more traditional activities. As the year progresses, they allot more time to curriculum integration.

Whatever route chosen, it is vital for teachers to allow students time to reflect. The reflection may be individual, small group, large group, written, spoken, or expressed in some other way. Reflection time is easy to overlook; but without it, students may not grasp the process of learning and the growing part they are playing in it.

Other thoughts on initiating curriculum integration are included in the response to Questions #14, "Does curriculum integration require a total team effort?" In addition, the exact procedure that Jim Beane and Barbara Brodhagen have used in working with students is outlined in the Appendix.

In summary, for curriculum integration to be meaningful for both the teachers and students, learning assumptions, classroom environment, and relationships must first be examined and new assumptions established. Reflection facilitates all three as well as sets up thoughtful practices for academic learning. The time spent addressing these issues will be well spent in establishing a firm foundation for curriculum integration. ⌘

5 Can the mandated curriculum be adequately addressed in curriculum integration?

Curriculum integration does not ignore or replace the mandated state or local curriculum, despite the assumptions of many. What does occur, however, is the rearrangement of the required content in a way that helps young people create meaning. James Beane (1995) confirmed this perspective, stating, "In the thoughtful pursuit of authentic curriculum integration, the disciplines of knowledge are not the enemy. Instead they are a useful and necessary ally" (p. 616). Another of the lessons learned by the two sixth grade teachers in Maine who instituted curriculum integration (Alexander, 1995) dealt with this issue. They state: "Traditional content can be incorporated within a student-oriented curriculum. In most areas we found that these sixth graders met or exceeded the content coverage of previous classes" (p. 56).

Accustomed to subject matter organization and trained to teach one or two subjects, teachers find it difficult to imagine how their content could be arranged in an equally or even more effective way. Those considering curriculum integration do have to take a leap of faith believing that students will learn the required content. Perhaps it is appropriate to first question the assumption that the traditional subject matter organization is the best way to acquire fundamental knowledge and skills. Certainly no evidence exists to support such an assumption.

As knowledge increases exponentially, courses of study, textbooks, and scope and sequence charts become overburdened with more knowledge and skills than any student (or adult, for that matter) can possibly learn in the given time. Students memorize enough to pass a test, but they are rarely given the opportunity to truly understand the complexity of topics or their application in the real world. With or without curriculum integration, educators and citizens must come to grips with the growing saturation of the curriculum.

In the meantime, educators must deal with the mandated curriculum or face professional jeopardy. Fortunately experience has confirmed that the required subject matter, in most cases, can be covered in curriculum integration or in conjunction with it. To help ensure this, the mandated curriculum should be clearly identified to both students and parents.

Teachers can post specific curriculum objectives and leave them up all year as a constant reminder of school and state expectations. As students help plan units and activities, they refer to the charts to determine if appropriate skills and knowledge are being included. When investigating a question about what homes are safest during a tornado or hurricane, two eighth grade boys decided to design and build a model house. As part of their plan, Josh and Lee listed the specific curriculum objectives they expected to include. They learned about weather, building construction, building materials and costs, geographic areas that may be susceptible to various natural disasters, and architectural design. In addition, they sharpened research and reading skills and learned to conduct effective interviews to find the information that they needed to answer their question. As part of the final project they wrote an essay on effective design. Through the one project, they had dealt with 15 objectives that covered math, social studies, language arts, and science.

In curriculum integration, not all students learn the same information at the same time or to the same degree. Therefore, teachers must also find a way to keep track of students' individual progress in the given curriculum. One way to do this is to make a list of curriculum objectives for each student exactly as they are written on the charts. Periodically, once every few weeks or as projects conclude, students review individual lists with teachers to determine which ones have been adequately learned. In most mandated curricula, some objectives should be mastered while others only need to be explored or reviewed. Such a distinction is helpful on the students' individual lists as well as on the curriculum posters.

In some cases mandated objectives just don't find a natural fit in curriculum integration themes. One objective that comes to mind is dividing fractions. This skill is part of almost every math curriculum, and yet applications in the real world are hard to find without considerable stretching. In a situation like this, lessons that don't fit into the plans developed by the teacher and class can be taught directly by the teacher. When teachers practice curriculum integration and are honest about the given curriculum, students voice little objection to learning a lesson on a specific objective that doesn't fit into their plans. Students sometimes even welcome a break from the demanding work of curriculum integration. In that way, the few curriculum "givens" that don't find a home in the themes can still be taught.

Math is a common concern in curriculum integration. Some teachers choose to teach math separately from the rest of the work. This may be more of a statement on the way we perceive and teach math than the disconnectedness of math from real purposes. In one eighth grade, all students learned algebra. This fit very well into curriculum integration when the teacher and students realized that algebra models real life situations. During one project, students raised money for their class trip by selling cookies. They sold the cookies on different days for various prices and kept data on prices charged and cookies sold. From these data they constructed an equation that predicted the optimum price to charge to make the maximum profit. As a follow-up lesson, they learned how to solve similar equations. Not only could they solve equations, but they could describe a situation in which it could be useful and, given a situation, could represent it algebraically. Mathematics can fit into curriculum integration but not necessarily as it is presented in a textbook.

Mandated curriculum can be very restrictive when it prescribes the order in which specific topics must be taught. Stringent requirements of sequence make curriculum integration very difficult. Most states, however, do not impose such restrictive and prescriptive standards on their educators. Georgia's Quality Core Curriculum, for instance, poses a challenge to meaningful curriculum, but not an obstacle. Teachers and students can reorganize the timing of these objectives and provide a more meaningful and challenging context for mastering these requirements. ⌘

> *The division into subjects and periods encourages a segmented rather than an integrated view of knowledge. Consequently, what students are asked to relate to in schooling becomes increasingly artificial, cut off from the human experiences subject matter is supposed to reflect.*
>
> — John Goodlad

6 Will students be handicapped on standardized tests or in mastering basic skills?

As explained in the previous question, teachers practicing curriculum integration incorporate strategies to ensure coverage of material needed to meet required objectives. Coverage and real learning, however, may be quite different matters. Both common educational sense and empirical evidence point to improved learning through curriculum integration.

All teachers seek to help students learn and curriculum integration teachers are no exception. They, however, are concerned with much more than academic growth for they are concerned about understanding democracy as a way of life, making connections to the world, and helping students understand themselves better. These concerns speak to the need for recognition and balance of student needs in education, not the neglect of academics. Basic skills comprise an important part of a student's learning, but only a portion.

Having a meaningful context not only contributes to students' learning basic skills, but goes beyond. Consider this example dealing with the objective of linear measuring. One class wrote a play to perform for parents and the school community. As part of the preparation, students had to plan and build a platform stage. With help from a carpenter they designed the stage, bought the wood, measured, and cut it. When putting the pieces together, they found the studs didn't quite fit together. The student-builders re-checked their measurements and discovered one piece that was measured incorrectly. Fortunately the stud was too long, so the mistake was easily corrected. Through the experience they learned not only how to measure correctly, but the effects of not measuring correctly and a context in which accurate measurement was essential. Along with many other skills and knowledge, the students learned in a rich context the basic skill of measurement.

Another example from a different subject area follows. Producing proper business letters is a common writing objective in the middle school curriculum. Traditionally, the teacher presents information about the parts of a business letter, students write a hypothetical business letter, and receive a grade on the product. In curriculum integration, however, learning to write a business letter takes on meaning beyond a grade. Determined to raise money for a village in El Salvador to help the villagers buy land, students planned a dance marathon and wanted to provide free snacks and prizes. They wrote to numerous area businesses to solicit donations. To do the job well and increase their chances for receiving donations, students knew the letters must be written error-free and in the proper format. The teacher reviewed the correct format and then helped them edit their letters. (Businesses donated enough prizes and food to last for 12 hours.) Students worked very hard to learn the skill of letter writing, not because it was required of them, but because it was an essential step in carrying out their plan.

There are many other examples to lend credibility to the contention that students learn the basic skills through this design. For many teachers and for those to whom teachers are accountable, standardized tests are more important than subjective success stories or contentions. Do students in curriculum integration perform adequately on tests such as the Iowa Test of Basic Skills? While extensive research is not yet available to answer this question, several curriculum integration teachers have examined test scores and found that their students learn the basic skills as well as or better than students in more traditional arrangements.

Elaine Homestead, a teacher in Georgia, compared ITBS scores for her team of students who participated in curriculum integration to the ITBS scores for the entire grade at her middle school. Although her team included none of the students identified as gifted, they scored better than the sixth grade students as a whole on all measures except math, which was taught separately.

Mark Springer (1994) and his colleague, Ed Silcox, have operated a whole learning or integrated curriculum "Watershed," with great success. Based on a dozen years' experience, these creators of this all-day program claim: "When we allow students' interests to drive the curriculum, rather than outmoded predetermined single-subject concerns, the students will respond with greater enthusiasm for learning which translates into greater achievement" (p. 129). After spending their entire seventh grade year in the Watershed project where they took no subjects or classes as such, these graduates, now eighth graders, had no academic problems and frequently displayed uncommon initiative and leadership.

While there is not yet a large body of evidence to determine how well students learn basic skills through curriculum integration, the evidence that does exist shows that students in curriculum integration score at least as well on standardized tests of basic skills as students in more traditional designs. Because skills are learned in a functional context students are much more likely to master and retain the skills of learning. ⌘

Martin Haberman claims good teaching is likely to be going on when students are:

- *Involved with issues they regard as vital;*
- *Engaged in exploring human differences;*
- *Planning what they will be doing;*
- *Applying ideals such as fairness, equity, or justice to their world;*
- *Doing an experiment, participating as an actor, or constructing things;*
- *Directly involved in a real life experience through field trips and interactions with resource people at work and in the community;*
- *Actively involved in heterogeneous groups that value divergent questioning strategies, multiple assignments in the same class, and activities that allow for alternative responses and solutions.*
- *Pushed to think about an idea in a way that questions common sense or a widely accepted assumption, compare, analyze, synthesize, evaluate, and generalize;*
- *Redoing, polishing or perfecting their work;*
- *Accessing information;*
- *Reflecting on their own lives and how they have come to believe what they do.— Phi Delta Kappan, 72 (4), 1991*

7 How does curriculum integration contribute to the goals of exploration and enrichment?

Curriculum integration by its very nature is both exploratory and enriching. Teachers and students are no longer restricted to covering a pre-planned and prescribed curriculum. As they seek out information and understandings, almost all the activities the teacher(s) and students pursue fall under the category of exploratory.

A major characteristic of young adolescents is their heightened curiosity, their sense of adventure. They ask, "How come?" "Why?" They probe; they experiment; they seek new fields to discover. Very few if any middle schools now adequately meet the exploratory needs of young adolescents. A cycle or two of required exploratory courses are very much in order, but they alone do not fulfill the need for new and varied experiences that young adolescents possess. In an open, integrated curriculum, however, the investigations carried out under the direction of academic team teachers lead students to areas of study beyond the basic four subject areas and call into play varied response techniques and skills; hence exploration and enrichment become characteristics of the general education block just as much as courses designated as exploratory.

Independent study is an age-old but seldom-used-in-school way of learning. The assumption exists that for students to learn they must have the constant direction of a teacher. In curriculum integration, however, individuals have opportunities to engage in independent study pursuing a particular topic or interest. The following two examples illustrate. During a project in which sixth grade students explored their own family trees and cultural heritage, one boy decided to do a photo collage of his living relatives. He borrowed a 35mm. camera and sought out instruction on how to take, develop, and print black and white photographs. His exploration included not only his family roots, but also the skills of photography. Another student of Asian descent explored the food of her culture. She collected family recipes and, along with her small group, cooked a traditional meal for the class. These examples illustrate how curriculum integration allows students to explore themselves and their interests while still staying within stated academic boundaries and enriching the class's study. In both cases there were many concomitant learnings in both the content and skill categories.

In short, when curriculum integration is implemented, the middle school will meet far more fully its responsibility to provide young adolescents with new, varied, and engaging information and experiences than has ever been the case with a discipline-based curriculum. ⌘

The late noted author James Michener was a teacher in one of the thirty experimental schools that were part of the Eight-Year Study. In later years he reflected on that teaching:

I watched with delight as my graduates earned highly successful places for themselves in both later college life and adult performance. I have always viewed with mild amusement the loose charges that Progressive Education was a failure or that it promoted laxity in either study or morals. My classes, if I say so myself, were among the best being taught in America at that time, all with a far above average model of deportment and learning. And through the years my former students constantly write to tell me that they evaluated those years in the same way. A failure? One of the greatest successes I've known.

As to the effect on me: it made me a liberal, a producer, a student of my world, a man with a point of view and the courage to exemplify it. I wish all students could have the experiences mine did. I wish all teachers could know the joy I found in teaching under such conditions.

— cited in *The Eight–Year Study Revisited: Lessons from the Past for the Present*

8 How can I secure adequate instructional resources?

Obviously, textbooks cannot suffice as the prime instructional resource when moving toward curriculum integration. Texts may be retained but they become *a* source of information not *the* source. The media center as it often does, can supply relevant references, and its resources will likely be exploited more thoroughly than has previously been the case. But the big difference in the area of resource materials is not only in *what* but *who*. The securing of appropriate resources and instructional materials is no longer the sole responsibility of the teacher. As emphasized in previous questions, curriculum integration puts the students actively in the center of the teaching / learning process. The students themselves, under the guidance of the teacher, discuss what kinds of information are needed to throw light on the problem at hand and then consider where such information might be found. Newspapers, magazines, and television programs all come into play. The students search the Internet, consider possible community resources, arrange interviews with resource persons, and write letters to various agencies and national organizations.

In many respects the search for information is a valid end in itself as a part of learning how to learn. The concomitant learnings that grow out of investigating resources, making contacts, and tapping varied printed, human, and technologically available information are many and of real importance as students become more independent learners. In addition, the experience of evaluating resources for reliability and appropriateness develops a valuable skill that is often part of state and local curricula / standards.

Two sixth grade teachers in rural Maine (Alexander, 1995) who took the initiative and successfully established an integrated curriculum during the year reached many important conclusions. Among them was this one:

> The community can provide abundant resources to enrich
> the school's program. All communities, even small rural ones,
> have valuable educational resources. They may take forms

other than traditional literary sources, but they are out there. These young people had developed a real capacity for locating and accessing community resources. They wrote to, called, and interviewed a great number of people in search of information.... They enticed many parents and other community members into contributing to their projects in a variety of ways. (p. 60)

Students will also share what they have discovered and learned, usually in both oral and written forms. In the process they become, in a real sense, teachers. And as the learning pyramid developed long ago made clear, the greatest degree of information retention is achieved when we teach others.

Since curriculum integration is a bottom up affair, it is not necessary that needed instructional materials be in hand before a new area of study is launched. In this aspect of teaching, as in so many others, curriculum integration calls for a paradigm shift. ⌘

LEARNING PYRAMID

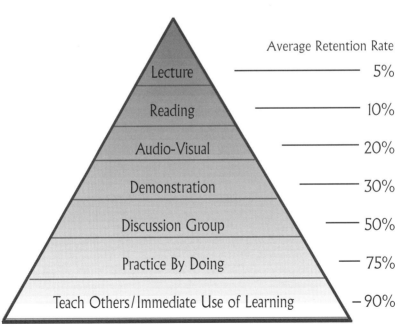

— *National Training Laboratories, Bethel, Maine*

9 How can I inform and involve parents?

How ow and when you involve and inform parents will be determined in part by the nature of the relationship with parents that already exists. Without the support of parents, however, curriculum integration will not easily reach its potential. Parents deserve to be active participants in their children's education and children deserve to have their parents involved. Since curriculum integration will be unfamiliar to parents, they are likely to be skeptical at first. Before and during implementing curriculum integration, therefore, parents need to be informed and involved at every turn.

Teachers and administrators can prepare parents in several ways. First preparations for parents may occur the year before their children will be participating in curriculum integration. A lot will depend upon whether one teacher or one team is implementing curriculum integration as opposed to several teams or an entire grade level. If parents have some choice in their children's placement, schools have the responsibility to inform parents so they can be involved in the choice perceived best for their child. In any case, schools can and should provide information about the philosophy and the practice of curriculum integration. Articles as free of educational jargon as possible should be made available. Evening meetings also allow parents the opportunity to be involved and have their concerns addressed long before their children reach the curriculum integration classroom.

When students have been assigned to specific classrooms or teams, new opportunities for parent involvement exist. Teachers can send letters home explaining their commitment to curriculum integration and set times to meet with groups of parents to discuss curriculum. These actions lead to the open relationships that will serve students, parents, and teachers well throughout the year.

Some teachers actually demonstrate the planning process with parents before using the same process with the children. Not only does this provide parents firsthand insights into the process but also eases parents' concerns about the seriousness of themes and incorporation of required subject matter. All this takes time but will build a yearlong partnership that pays off handsomely in involvement and student achievement.

Parents will be primarily concerned about whether or not their children will learn the required curriculum and be adequately prepared for the next level of schooling. The parent letter on page 24 speaks volumes on this point. Teachers can allay valid concerns through constant communication and by sharing that responsibility with the students themselves. In addition to the standard conferences, report cards, and calls home, students may write their parents periodically explaining recent activities, their progress, curriculum objectives that have been met, and projections for upcoming activities. Through such a report, students not only communicate what they are learning but also reflect on the process of their learning. With this sort of preparation, students also become very capable of leading student-parent conferences.

In curriculum integration, students undertake projects that result in such things as posters, displays, performances, art work, and various forms of printed materials. Students enjoy sharing their creations, and inviting parents in to view and discuss these projects, providing more interaction among students, teachers, and parents.

In addition to being informed about their children's progress, parents play an important role in the classroom itself. Curriculum integration requires resources beyond the classroom and school library, and parents possess diverse experiences and expertise that may be invaluable to the ongoing study. At the beginning of the year, teachers and/or students may survey parents to find areas of expertise present as well as determine their willingness to work with students. Some parents may work with the entire class while others may prefer to assist small groups or individuals. Teachers understand, of course, that not all parents will be able to directly participate in class activities but they may suggest experts in the community who could contribute.

Parents are their children's first teachers and also the primary experts on their own children. Their feedback on their children's progress and observations about classroom happenings can provide teachers with beneficial insights. Asking parents for real feedback is a scary proposition for most teachers, and without some established relationship, it is even more difficult. Much of the threat, however, dissolves in mutual respect when interaction, openness, and honesty characterize the relationship. Not all feedback will be positive, and it shouldn't be so, but it will most likely be sincere and thoughtful. Fully including parents in their children's experiences in curriculum integration means teachers must be open to honest criticism as well as to praise.

Parental feedback comes at various times and in diverse ways — from conferences, questionnaires sent home, meetings with small groups of parents, telephone calls, and impromptu visits before or after school. However solicited and received, the reactions of parents sincerely given and openly accepted can only add to the positive impact of curriculum integration. ⌘

...Thanks so much for all the wonderful things you are doing with our children this year! Josh really seems to feel that he's taking control of his own learning, which is precisely what he needs for high school!!

I'm puzzled by the parents who continue to wonder if their kids are getting what they'll need for future learning environments. I wonder why they're that concerned!! Perhaps because we've had a child in high school, we know that Josh will be well-prepared in the important things — and the other things he'll learn to deal with somehow!

Your approach to curriculum development takes the idea of student involvement in its development further than any classroom Josh has been in, but this seems particularly appropriate for the last year at middle school.

Keep up the good work!

Warmly,
Meg McCann

10 How does curriculum integration change my role as a teacher?

Inherent in the middle school concept itself and certainly in curriculum integration is a major change in the teacher's role. It involves shifting from an instructor to a director of learning, from sole authority to facilitator, from giver of knowledge to organizer of learning activities, from talker to listener and observer.

Perhaps the most difficult adjustment for teachers who have been successful is giving up control. Throughout preservice training and inservice evaluations, teachers constantly receive the message that they must be in control of both student learning and behavior. To contemplate relinquishing that control is frightening. Behavior expectations and consequences are now open for discussion. The teacher can no longer plan exactly what will occur the day after tomorrow, let alone fill out a detailed plan book a week ahead of time. Flexibility becomes more important than predictability. Control and responsibility are shared with students. The teacher assists students in making good decisions rather than telling them what is presumably the best way. This new role requires a belief in young people and faith in the precept that middle school students can and will become seriously engaged in learning.

School experiences have revolved around the teacher as "the fountain of wisdom." A popular school adage, *Knowledge provided here. Bring your own container,* implies students as passive recipients of teachers' knowledge. This role limits teachers to sharing knowledge they already possess. In curriculum integration the teacher's role necessarily changes as students investigate questions to which the teacher has no specific answer; for instance, "Will technology eventually kill us?" or "Why is there so much violence in the world?" Certainly teacher expertise can assist students in planning an effective way to seek answers to such questions, but no college course addressed the specific content of these concerns. Teachers must facilitate students in finding the needed information rather than communicating already-in-hand or in-mind knowledge.

Becoming a facilitator rather than a provider of knowledge also changes the teacher's role outside of the classroom. Most teachers have had the experience of spending hours researching and preparing a unit, only to find that it failed miserably when the unit met the harshness of student disinterest. Curriculum integration includes the students in planning, so the teacher is no longer solely responsible for ensuring creative, active learning. Teachers will still spend time outside of class planning mini-lessons, locating resource persons, meeting with other teachers to gain advice or assistance, framing questions that need to be addressed or reflecting on the progress and involvement of classes and individuals, but not planning content in the absence of learners.

When the teachers completely control the classroom environment, they must constantly talk to convey their vision of learning. As teachers share the control in the classroom, so too must they share the floor. No longer is the adult opinion the only one of import. Teachers now listen to students in order to understand them and facilitate the learning of the class.

The other side of listening is observing. When practicing curriculum integration, teachers can watch for student frustration and withdrawal as well as involvement and growth. They become sensitive to nuances in whole class discussions, small group interactions, and individual responses. In a classroom where the teacher runs the class, few such opportunities for observing exist. As teachers step back and students take on some responsibility, teachers can observe what's going on in the classroom.

In curriculum integration, teachers spend a great deal of time talking *with* students rather than *to* them, guiding them in their school experiences rather than remaining an emotionally distant adult. When the timing is right, students will place their concerns and themselves out on the table for others to examine. It becomes impossible for teachers to deal only with academic concerns while ignoring the other concerns of young persons. In one unit entitled "Teen Issues," students were concerned about eating disorders, and it was eventually revealed that some class members evidenced signs of anorexia and bulimia. The teachers in this unit could not continue teaching the science and psychology of eating disorders while ignoring individual students who were struggling with the consequences. They had to serve as primary advisors when the problem was first noticed and then refer the individuals to the school counselor. Not all teacher guidance is so dramatic, but in curriculum integration, teachers work daily with individual interests and concerns, weaving individual involvement into class goals.

Curriculum integration teachers inevitably find themselves in the role of adviser. Because those in small teams spend more time with individuals they become true advocates for their students. Most teachers do truly care about students but don't have the time or a meaningful context in which to develop the personal relationships and understandings of students needed to be advocates for their needs. Curriculum integration teachers have a better chance to form that kind of relationship.

In addition to speaking for the needs of students, teachers may find themselves in the position of critically examining many school practices. Curriculum integration is all but impossible to practice in 50 minute periods with 120 different students, and quiet classrooms don't necessarily mean real learning is taking place. Teachers who seek to practice curriculum integration face such realities. They have to work around obstacles or try to remove them. Some do both. These are the teachers who can accept the role of change agent within their team, school, and community.

Professional relationships may change as well. Some curriculum integration teachers lead other teachers in searching for meaningful curriculum. Other teachers may find themselves alone in their efforts. Often the reaction to innovative teachers is determined by administrators or other teachers and has little to do with the curriculum integration teachers themselves. By consciously considering the issue of professional relationships, integration teachers may be able to influence professional relationships or be more accepting when they have little control over those relationships.

When practicing curriculum integration, the teacher's role thus changes considerably in the classroom and in relationships outside the classroom. Changes are uncomfortable, but with the support of students and a firm belief in the practice, teachers who become involved in curriculum integration have a unique opportunity for personal and professional growth — and their sense of professional efficacy will increase. ⌘

> *We need to break the illusion of separate subjects. Education is about life. Life is a fabric of relationships...the child should grasp this through his experience. Subjects which break off areas of knowledge and set up as independent islands have deceptive powers. Traditional teaching of subjects...is death to the understanding.* — Peter Abb, 1966

11 How does the student's role change in curriculum integration?

Teachers often lament that their students do not take responsibility for their learning. And yet, students are rarely given real responsibility. Their role in learning is largely confined to doing the assigned work and behaving according to the rules. Teachers may allow students to decide from several ways of doing a book report or choose how they want to represent the solar system, but these are not substantial choices, ones that require students to think seriously about how they can best learn important concepts. Curriculum integration assists them in developing real understandings and in becoming responsible for their own learning and behavior.

As students begin their work in curriculum integration, they are likely to be puzzled by the privilege and the responsibility of making significant decisions. At first, they can't believe that the teacher really means for them to have so much input. Many times they have been asked for their opinion only to have it ignored or considered lightly. As they realize the real opportunities, students take their decisions very seriously and appreciate the individual power involved in reaching consensus.

One class spent 45 minutes at the beginning of the year debating whether they wanted three or four class monitors. Even when most of the class had settled on three monitors one student, Will, insisted on four. Will, who had exhibited many behavior difficulties in school, was simply testing the sincerity of the teacher's intention to listen to students. The class decided to try three monitors for a week, four the next week, and then revisit the issue. Will understood that his voice really did count and refrained from similar stand-offs the rest of the year.

Students soon learn which decisions are critical to their learning and which are merely procedural. They then spend less time making decisions while making better choices. Students realize that for most decisions only a handful of individuals have strong opinions and others can agree to several possible resolutions. In addition, they understand that "agree" can mean anything from living with to loving a class decision.

Through curriculum integration, students become supporters of each other rather than competitors. Class goals are met through individual, small group, and whole class activities. To meet them, students must work with each and every student at some point and all contribute an important piece. Where students previously looked for and dwelled on each other's weaknesses, the ideal of common goals necessitates looking for and using the strengths of their peers. Competition makes progress toward some goals difficult, even unachievable. With teacher guidance, students quickly recognize the power of cooperation and become adept at using it.

Recognition of individual strengths lends a realistic aspect to cooperative learning. Traditionally successful students tend to look for a direct route to a quick solution and possess the skills to travel that route. However, they become frustrated when that path meets a dead end. Students who have more difficulty finding success in school often possess the skill of looking for alternative paths to the same end and do not expect find a fast solution. When typically successful students do not have a ready answer, others help them examine possibilities.

Possibly for the first time, students have to truly listen to one another. In order to reach consensus, students must understand and consider every person's opinion. Eventually students speak from their sincere concerns and interests and toward the progress of the class, opening a part of themselves that previously did not come into play in school.

Having common goals, recognizing individual strengths, and listening to all contributions help develop a caring community of learners. Caring even moves beyond classroom goals. For instance, in one sixth grade class, Heather was painfully shy and slow to think and respond to other people. Her lack of social skills and insecurity contributed to her frequent absences. At the beginning of the year in which she participated in curriculum integration, her classmates were not cruel to her but neither did they particularly pay attention to her or her needs. After several months of working together, however, other students made sure that Heather was included in groups and that her opinion was sought (even though she still chose not to respond at times). The kindness extended onto the playground and the bus. Young adolescents can be extremely kind and caring, given an atmosphere free of competition and the opportunity for everyone to participate and succeed in pursuing common class goals.

After the initial adjustment to real involvement, almost all students appreciate the opportunity to participate. A few, however, resist the change. Students who have been successful in the traditional class are most often the resistors. They are the ones who already had figured out the game of school and could win at it. They know how to listen, absorb, and spit knowledge back with a minimum of work and maximum of results (i.e. good grades). They are comfortable with the school that produces a hierarchy of winners and losers, since they are accustomed to being winners. Curriculum integration, on the other hand, requires them to think about matters that have no ready answers and calls for them to cooperate instead of compete with their peers. They are expected to help others as well as develop their own skills and talents. Over time, most successful students understand and appreciate the new approach, but a select few may continue to resist.

One such student was Manuel, an 8th grader who received nothing less than A's throughout his school career. He entered 8th grade fully expecting his teachers to tell him what he needed to learn. He was ready to do that and thereby collect his A's. Throughout the year, Manuel wanted to work by himself instead of in groups. He begged the teacher to just tell him what he needed to know so that he could earn good grades. He longed to just take a test instead of having to apply new knowledge to a school or community project. The teacher accommodated his needs to the best of her ability within the parameters of curriculum integration. She gave him tests and allowed him to work by himself whenever appropriate. She could not, however, provide easy answers to the class's complex questions nor could she assure Manuel that he would be part of an elite group who could earn the highest grades. He never fully adjusted and appreciated the goals and practice of curriculum integration.

On the other end of the spectrum are students who haven't been able to find success in school, no matter how good their intentions or sincere their efforts. Curriculum integration offers unique hope for these students. They become integral parts of a learning community with peers and an adult who listens to their ideas. They find support from other students for achieving their academic and personal growth. School and learning take on new meanings as students investigate questions that relate to their lives and concerns.

Andy was such a student. He had a diagnosed learning disability, struggled with issues of sexuality, and often misbehaved in school. After some initial skepticism, Andy placed his faith in curriculum integration and the teacher who was trying it for the first time. By November he became a class leader, well respected by his peers for his creativity, hard work, artistic abilities, and expert presentations. He found and arranged for guest speakers, located numerous resources, and volunteered to work way beyond the requirements in both time and quality. Andy even led his classmates in making presentations about curriculum integration to teachers across the state. (Andy, incidentally, graduated from high school in June 1999 and is now attending college.)

Not all students show this much growth in a year of curriculum integration. A few may fail as they did in traditional designs. Teachers of curriculum integration observe, however, that most students who previously had trouble making connections to school find important connections to both learning, themselves, and their classmates through meaningful, inclusive curriculum.

In summary, the role of students certainly takes new directions under curriculum integration. The new role centers around participating actively, accepting responsibility for their own learning and behavior, and collaborating with others. Almost all students accept these new roles enthusiastically, and the increased personal and academic growth that results warrants the efforts. ⌘

An early version of the first principle of the highly successful *Foxfire* approach states:

All the work teachers and students do together must flow from student desire, student concerns. It must be infused from the beginning with student choice, design, revision, execution, reflection, and evaluation. Teachers, of course, are still responsible for assessing the ministering to their students' developmental needs.

Most problems that arise during classroom activities must be solved in collaboration with students. When one asks, "Here's a situation that just came up. I don't know what to do about it. What should I do?" the teacher turns that question back to the class to wrestle with and solve, rather than simply answering it. Students are trusted continually, and all are led to the point where they embrace responsibility.

12 What instructional strategies are needed in curriculum integration?

In addition to being a philosophy and a design, curriculum integration is also an instructional strategy. It is a comprehensive way of using various teaching and learning approaches that feature teachers and students collaboratively deciding on both ends and means.

To illustrate a commonly used strategy, consider this example: In a unit on growing up, a few of the questions students generated in the areas identified were:

Biology / Disorders
>   Why do people have to go through adolescence?
>   What is the role of genetics?

Self as Part of Community
>   How will I fit in with my friends when I get older?
>   How will my relationship with my parents change?
>   How can I make a difference?

Self (Me)
>   Why do we do the things we do, good and bad?
>   How am I going to do in high school?
>   What type of job will be best for me?

Growing Up in Different Cultures
>   Are we grown up after 18 years?
>   Will I be able to make a living?

How Your Past Affects Your Future
>   How long will we live?
>   Why am I who I am?

Because of the depth of each of the concepts, students decided to divide into groups to explore different concepts. The groups varied in size from three to five members. With the assistance of teachers, members of each group planned how to answer their questions and who in the group would be responsible for which part. These cooperative groups had the essential components of individual accountability and group goals, but were not assigned by the teacher in an arbitrary manner to make sure all were involved. Students worked cooperatively to solve their problem of seeking answers to questions.

Small group learning was the overarching strategy for this unit; but it was recognized that to answer some of the questions would require a few formal presentations and mini-lessons. For example, students certainly did not have an adequate background in genetics to even begin to explore the effects of genetics on their lives. Teachers, therefore, prepared a half-hour lecture covering the basics of genetics and followed with discussions exploring issues such as genetic diseases and predisposition to addictions. These particular lectures were given only to the group studying biology and disorders, but the unit also included some large group presentations.

One topic that intrigued all the students was personality types. After receiving some information about personality formation, students invited the school counselor in to discuss and then administer the Myers-Briggs inventory. This instrument helped students understand their preferences and how different preference types interact. Scientific investigations were also utilized in the unit. The group that studied genetics set up an experiment to breed one black and one white mouse. They predicted the color of the offspring for each generation based on what they had learned and then recorded data on the actual outcomes. Students dealing with the question about how they would do in high school developed and distributed a survey to high school freshmen. They analyzed the data collected and presented to the entire group their findings about the attributes needed to succeed in high school.

The search for information took many forms. All groups visited both school and city libraries. They also searched the Internet and visited high schools and community centers. One group interviewed local psychologists and psychiatrists to better understand personality development and the emotional and social components of growing up. All students interviewed parents and grandparents, where available, to investigate changing parent-child relationships.

Peer teaching was another strategy employed. Because various groups concentrated on different topics, they had to share their information, skills, and insights with the rest of the class. Sharing usually took the form of group presentations that included lecturettes, small group activities, clips of movies and documentaries, games, reflections, and hypothetical problem solving. Within the groups, one or two students might do the research or interview an expert and then teach the rest of the group what they had learned. Students found that they could learn as much from one another as they could from teachers. Presentations of the small groups to the whole class were certainly interactive. It was, of course, still the teacher's ultimate responsibility to ensure that an adequate body of information was included.

Strategies utilized rarely included worksheets or answering questions from a textbook, although if those were deemed helpful in reaching stated goals, they would be included.

Clearly teachers must have an extensive repertoire of instructional strategies. They have to assist in designing experiments, refining surveys, locating resources, inventing games, resolving conflicts, analyzing data, and delegating responsibility. In addition, they deliver appropriate lectures, organize parts of the unit, monitor student involvement, and assess learning on a daily basis. Teachers also have to create strategies for activities and learning they cannot possibly anticipate. Along with their students, curriculum integration teachers are continually learning new content and refining various instructional approaches.

Many strategies used in curriculum integration, it should be recognized, are the traditional ones. The reasons they are selected, however, may be quite different. In curriculum integration, strategies and activities selected result from student-teacher planning rather than teachers' unilateral decisions.

As they collaborate in developing plans, students learn what activities are best in what situation. They realize that one strategy does not work for every situation. Perhaps surprisingly, they appreciate the value of a lecture when it is placed in the context of meaningful questions. For students to become lifelong learners, the skill of choosing an appropriate strategy is essential. They need to know when to consult books, when to seek experts, and when they need more formal instruction.

Curriculum integration itself is a comprehensive strategy that utilizes many instructional techniques. Because responsibility for selecting means to answer questions rests partly with students, they too learn the value and place of various instructional approaches and ways of learning. In short, they learn how to learn. ⌘

13 How is student progress assessed and reported?

T he inadequacy of traditional ABC grading procedures has increasingly been recognized by educators and even by many parents. Changes, however haltingly, are beginning to appear as supplements to the well-entrenched but limited grading and reporting system. When curriculum integration holds sway, major changes in the ways student progress is assessed are necessary and inevitable.

Since the objectives of curriculum integration go far beyond the acquisition of prescribed content, the basis for evaluating students' performances must follow suit. Attention is now given to the processes utilized in learning and not just to the product, which is usually a test or report that presumably fairly represents one's learning. One's status in acquiring desired behavioral attributes becomes a significant component in the evaluation process. So too does the demonstrated ability to apply skills in solving problems.

The authentic assessment movement now underway gets a big boost when teams move to integrate the curriculum. Perhaps the most fundamental and significant change comes about as students assume responsibility for monitoring and assessing their learning. They help set the objectives, establish the criteria for evaluation, reflect on their work through journals and portfolios, and discuss with peers and teachers their progress. Gone largely is the cutthroat competition that requires losers in order to have winners. Grading, as such, gives way to assessing the progress of individuals toward known and agreed-upon objectives. One's achievement at a particular point in time does not have to be summarized (or squeezed) into a single letter or numerical grade. There are, instead, several evidences of effort, progress, and achievement available. These may include notes taken in a research effort, a checklist of specific objectives completed as a self-evaluation, a picture of the diorama created by the student that was displayed in the local mall, the comments of a teacher on a draft of an essay, the completed rubric used in evaluating an oral report, and, still an appropriate part of a comprehensive assessment of progress, one might find a graded test of information acquired. Still other kinds of evidence depending on the nature of the activities undertaken will be available; but there will always be significantly more information than the grade derived from scores on paper and pencil tests and completed homework assignments.

In typical classroom situations the completion of homework assignments is a major factor in determining grades. In fact, failure to complete homework is the single greatest cause of failing grades. Homework, like grading itself, desperately needs to be revisited whether or not a team is employing curriculum integration. Viewed by students as busy work, it builds negative attitudes toward school and education itself. *Homework,* the word itself, has become pejorative and is often spoken disdainfully. The matter of homework also appears to be a no-win situation with parents. Roughly half of them complain because their children are over-burdened with assignments while another substantial segment question why their children don't have more homework.

In curriculum integration the one uniform assignment for all disappears, voiding that all-too-often truism, "What is everybody's business is nobody's business." With different students or small groups pursuing different aspects of the theme and utilizing different information sources, seldom will all students be asked to do the same assignment. Rather than the kind of homework students view negatively — answering questions at the end of a text chapter or completing practice exercises — students in a class that is seeking to integrate learning in a democratic context are more likely to pursue out-of-class learning activities that may require more than one night or one hour or utilizing a single source. Interviewing adults, analyzing television programs, working with classmates constructing a project, or seeking information on a particular concept of the theme from the Internet are examples of the kind of out-of-class learning activities students might undertake.

Report card time is likely to have students writing a letter to their parents providing a narrative assessment of their work to accompany the impersonal system-wide card, holding a student-led parent conference, or participating in an evening activity put on by the class to share with parents and families what they have learned. The kinds of assessment utilized display little of the comparisons that are inevitable in the ABC system. Students have no need to compete; they are engaged actively in assessing their own progress, reflecting on their achievements, and setting goals for the weeks ahead. ⌘

14 Does curriculum integration require a total team effort?

A total team commitment to implement curriculum integration would be highly desirable. Ideal circumstances might be a two-person team or even a single teacher with a substantial block of time. Only rarely, however, does the ideal situation exist. On some teams only one or two members may want to try curriculum integration. But curriculum integration can be accomplished by one teacher who believes strongly in the philosophy — if that teacher has sufficient support. If two teachers on a four- or five-person team are interested in implementing curriculum integration, a logical step would be to form a team of their own. However, if reorganization of the staff is not possible, a pair of teachers can practice curriculum integration while the remainder of the team and school continue as usual. Practicing curriculum integration under these circumstances is certainly more of a challenge, but not an impossibility.

Some teachers ease their way into curriculum integration by increasingly including the students in curriculum planning and other classroom decisions, an appropriate approach. Other teachers decide to jump in with both feet. On the first day of school students can start deciding classroom guidelines, prompted by the questions "What makes a good learning experience?" and "What are the responsibilities of students and teachers?" After laying the foundations for learning and classroom expectations, the class can move onto academic concerns with the same degree of student involvement.

In one case the teacher had decided ahead of time that the first unit would center around the theme of conflict. This was admittedly a deviation from Beane's recommendation, but starting with a given theme did not preclude significant student input from that point on.

Based on what she had learned in a *Foxfire* class, the teacher guided each group of students in planning using six questions: *What do you know about the topic? What do you think you know? What do you want to know? How will you learn it? How will you and others know that you learned it? What will you do with your new knowledge and skills?* Students knew from the beginning both the social studies and math requirements for the year, so as they planned they included appropriate knowledge and skills from the required lists as well as many that were not listed.

When answering the first two questions, students generally stayed within the subject area of social studies. In addressing the question, What do you want to know? the theme of conflict moved well beyond the boundaries of traditional social studies. They formed guiding questions about wars and conflicts including *How do conflicts start? How can they be avoided? What are the important events leading to conflict? What are the environmental impacts of wars? What can we do to ease the suffering from wars?* and *What lessons does this have for my life?* With the guiding questions in hand, students divided into groups, each group studying a different war. After gathering information from many and varied sources and synthesizing answers to their questions, groups presented their information and conclusions to the whole class. After that, each class synthesized more general answers to their guiding questions and decided what they could do with their new learning.

Through this one "social studies" unit, students learned science and technology by studying the environmental impact of wars and investigating weapons development. Math skills were brought into play in understanding charts, statistics, and demographic data. Reading and writing were used throughout the unit in doing research, reading about various wars, writing letters for information, and writing journals, stories, and poems. Guidance or personnel development functions were also served by learning strategies to resolve personal conflicts.

The process described here is one possibility for moving toward curriculum integration within the boundaries of one or two subject area classes. When talking to other pioneering teachers, one may find many variations on planning with students. The underlying commitment to involve students in a curriculum that has meaning for their lives, however, remains the same.

While conducting the conflict unit the social studies/math teacher described above repeatedly invited the other teachers on the team to participate in various ways. Each invitation was just that, it wasn't a demand for them to help, nor a judgment on what teachers chose to do in their own classrooms. When students needed to write a formal letter, the teacher of language arts willingly took time to hone the students' composition skills. The science teacher also assisted students in understanding the environmental effects of wars.

Some educators question the wisdom of one teacher within a team treating curriculum and students in a manner different from other teachers. Students, they say, shouldn't have to adjust to one kind of environment in one classroom and something different in another. Young people, however, are adept at perceiving and responding to various teachers, situations, and expectations. They adjust all the time in most schools as they move from class to class and teacher to teacher. Even when rules and expectations are the same over several classrooms or even the whole school, teachers are individuals with varying personalities who deal with students in their own way. Curriculum integration by itself neither magnifies nor diminishes those individual differences among teachers.

Further, curriculum integration provides a forum for students to examine expectations in different situations and learn better how to deal with them. As long as students don't talk about or disparage individual teachers, they can discuss various expectations and how they, individually and as a group, can learn effectively in all situations.

In summary, curriculum integration can be practiced in less than ideal situations. While challenging, it is not impossible. It is important, however, for the teacher(s) who decides to try curriculum integration to inform all parties who may have an interest in those students and to repeatedly invite others to participate. At the same time, the curriculum integration teacher must maintain a professional mutual respect with nonparticipating teammates and colleagues. ⌘

Almost everyone has had occasion to look back upon his school days and wonder what has become of the knowledge he was supposed to have amassed during his years of schooling, and why it is that the technical skills he acquired have to be learned over again in changed form in order to stand him in good stead. Indeed, he is lucky who does not find that in order to make progress, in order to go ahead intellectually, he does not have to unlearn much of what he learned in school.

— John Dewey, 1938

15 How does curriculum integration meet students' individual needs?

T eachers bear the challenging responsibility of meeting the widely varying needs of individuals. In classrooms where teachers are the center of instruction and students do the same work at the same time in the same way, individuals are not really served, rather it is the class that is taught. Meeting individual needs is a huge burden and calls for a tremendous amount of extra work for the teacher. Cultural differences also must be addressed, which is difficult and usually contrived in a group mentality. Classes may spend a few days on various cultures here and there, studying generalizations and stereotypes but neglecting individual variations within a culture.

Curriculum integration, however, increases the opportunity to recognize individuals, their distinct backgrounds, strengths, and needs. Students bring themselves, in all their complexities, to the planning process. When investigating the query "Will we ever stop killing each other?" the activities could take numerous directions and cover much content. Because they choose from several options, students' individual and group interests are major factors in decisions.

In the unit, *Growing Up,* students identified a number of novels about how young adolescents dealt with adversity. One of the books was *Night* by Elie Wiesel. In it he describes his young adolescent experiences in the Auschwitz concentration camp. Jewish students chose that book because the Holocaust was an important part of their history. Other students joined as well to learn more about both the Holocaust and the Jewish faith. Another novel, *Roll of Thunder, Hear My Cry* by Mildred Taylor, about the experience of an African American family before the Civil Rights Act of 1964 was of particular interest to others. All students were able to find at least one book that interested them.

The practice of achieving consensus in curriculum integration also assures that individual needs will be recognized fairly. No person's opinion may be excluded, since the group plan must include every individual's interests to some degree. Individuals bring their own interests as well as their cultural understanding and knowledge to be factored into the class plan. Without consensus, students generally might be well served; but there are always a few who, lacking any part in the decisions, refuse to commit to the activity.

Students also have opportunities to express their individual interests and strengths in small group sessions. For instance, in a group investigating the Vietnam conflict, various individuals chose to specialize in weapons development, important political decisions, protests, music at home, or effects on Vietnamese people. After conducting individual and group investigations, the class came together to paint a rich picture of the conflict. Throughout the work at various times they paired up, worked as a whole group, and/or helped individuals needing assistance.

In heterogeneous classrooms it is difficult to meet individual needs, especially when students range from the gifted to the functionally illiterate. Under curriculum integration, accommodation is not quite so difficult. In one unit, two students actually read Freud, Skinner, and Piaget to learn about adolescent development, while another student read children's picture books to discover the cultural messages they contained. None of these three students was singled out because every student, with teacher guidance, could adjust the work to his or her ability. Every student, in essence, is assisted in developing an individual educational plan.

As with the process, the product can also be individualized. Some students excel at writing, while others' strengths may be in speaking, art, graphic representation, or the performing arts. In preparing to share with the whole class, a group can incorporate varied skills in an effective presentation depending on the strengths of the group members. At the same time, working together also allows students to share and use their strengths in teaching others.

Curriculum integration provides the context for gaining familiarity with students. As students work in small groups or individually, teachers have a chance to interact with individuals, discover their strengths and challenges, their involvement or reticence, and view their effective or ineffective relationships with others. Aaron, for instance, usually appeared to be very busy. After talking with him, however, the teacher discovered that he knew virtually nothing about his topic. Aaron could read and write adequately, but was an expert at appearing to be busy while actually doing nothing. Aaron and the teacher agreed on a plan whereby he checked in with the teacher on a regular basis until he learned to monitor himself. Another student, Erica, worked hard but learned little. The teacher discovered that she read very poorly. As a result the teacher suggested strategies for better comprehension as well as more appropriate books.

Curriculum integration allows teachers to assist students in meeting their individual needs because the learning centers on the students instead of an impersonal curriculum. Since the class does not revolve around the actions of the teachers, teachers have time to work with individual students and effectively guide them. As teachers let go of the assumption that teaching calls for all students to participate in the same way, they take an important step toward meeting the needs of individuals. Curriculum integration requires that that assumption be put aside. ⌘

> *What is to be learned cannot be foreign to individual nature. Books can include but a small portion of any true curriculum. Since the content of the curriculum consists essentially of solutions to problems, the child must first feel something of the problem and be placed where he can most adequately live the solution provided. This means that the school must take on more of the characteristics of life itself.*
>
> • • • • •
>
> *In the case where no purpose is present, there the weak and foolish teacher has often in times past, cajoled and promised and sugar–coated, and this we all despise. Purpose then — its presence or absence — exactly distinguishes the desirable ...interest from the mushy type of anything–to–keep–the–dear–things–interested or amused. It is purpose then that we want, worthy purposes, urgently sought. Get these, and the interest will take care of itself.*
>
> *— William Heard Kilpatrick, 1919*

16 What is the role of the principal in curriculum integration?

The key role of the principal in determining a school's success is unquestioned. No one person has more influence on the climate and culture of a school than does the principal. This is a particularly critical truism when the school or some of its faculty seek to reach beyond interdisciplinary or multidisciplinary curriculum designs. Without the moral support, demonstrated in both verbal and non-verbal ways, of the chief administrator, teachers are not likely to be the risk takers they must be when seeking to practice integrated curriculum.

However anxious a school leader may be to get the faculty to move beyond interdisciplinary teaming, demanding it via an administrative fiat is not the way to go. Encourage, support, suggest, *yes;* but require, *no.* A first step for the progressive administrator is to become knowledgeable about curriculum integration. Read Beane's works (1993, 1997), the stories of successful efforts (Alexander, 1995; Springer, 1995; Pate, Homestead, & McGinnis, 1997), and other advocates of integrated curriculum (Vars, 1993; Brazee & Capelluti, 1994). In addition, sample theme issues of journals (*Middle School Journal,* November 1991, January 1992, September, 1996, March 1998, November 1998; *Educational Leadership,* October 1991, April 1995). Further sources are provided in Question 20.

Only when the principal is comfortable discussing the theory, is fully aware of the barriers likely to be faced, and is genuinely enthusiastic about the possibilities of curriculum integration can he or she provide needed support, such as adjusting schedules, gathering resources, and communicating with other faculty, parents, and community.

First efforts by a team to implement curriculum integration may prove disappointing. Students who have been conditioned to be compliant may not accept the opportunity to share in the decision making. The administrator can listen as the team members express their disappointment, assure them that this is to be expected, and help them think through what can be done to help make a further effort successful. Temporary failure should not only be permitted but expected and seen as a learning experience. Maintaining the offensive is critical to ultimate success.

The administrator of a middle school that includes some teachers or teams seeking to implement curriculum integration might want to share information about the plans with the central office and the superintendent both in advance and during the process. If the superintendent is approached by a concerned parent and unable to give a proper response for lack of information the project could be in jeopardy. It is expected, of course, that the principal will have checked with the team to be sure that parents have been fully informed. The principal might also communicate directly with the parents. Of course, only time spent in the classroom will yield the perspective the principal needs to understand, appreciate, and evaluate the efforts of a team seeking to achieve curriculum integration.

The basis for teacher evaluation will need to be altered so as to reflect the initiative, professional commitment, and personal risk taken by those who venture into curriculum integration. Curriculum integration classrooms operate on different premises than more traditional approaches. Teacher evaluations that center on the teacher as giver of knowledge who follows a prescribed lesson format ignore many of the learning processes of curriculum integration. Expecting detailed lesson plans a week in advance is unrealistic when decisions are shared with students. If administrators desire to support teachers willing to take the risk of progressing toward curriculum integration, teacher evaluation procedures have to undergo significant changes. Improved student attitude toward school, reduced absenteeism, and fewer discipline referrals are indicators of success that will likely occur but not be included in conventional supervisory evaluations that focus on the public performance of a teacher. ⌘

> *...the answers to a problem in one so-called subject area often surface more readily when viewed from the perspective of some other so-called subject area. Every good teacher knows this is true; as do scientists, business executives, artists, and just about everyone faced with a real life problem. Why, then, should we impose an unreal, artificial structure on an all too real process?*
>
> — Mark Springer in *Watershed: A Successful Voyage into Integrative Learning,*

17 What instructional organization plan is needed to support curriculum integration?

Schools for young adolescents use various instructional plans to present the curriculum. The typical junior high school organization arranges instruction by subject area departments while middle schools for the most part organize around instructional teams of two to five teachers. Curriculum integration is much more easily accomplished in small teams where fewer students spend more time with fewer teachers.

Curriculum integration requires scheduling flexibility. And when there are many different teachers involved, attempts to be flexible meet with complications. Consider this: one teacher and a group of students need three hours to work on a project, but are scheduled for only an hour together. In a departmentalized arrangement, it would be almost impossible to rearrange the schedule because that one teacher would have to consult all the teachers who share any students with him/her anytime in those three hours. Adjusting the schedule in such an organization is similar to figuring out a complex logic puzzle but more complicated because the pieces are people with their own plans and personalities.

Even on teams of four or five it can be difficult to be flexible. A teacher who needs extra time has the advantage of common planning time and a shared group of students but still has to find a way to juggle two or three classes of students. Certainly it can be done when all the teachers on the team cooperate, but it still must be planned well in advance of the needed time. In curriculum integration, however, the need for an expanded period may not be known days in advance. On the more desirable two-teacher team, flexibility becomes possible as needed. It's relatively easy to quickly confer in the hall and arrange for an extra amount of time with a certain group of students knowing exactly where the other students will be.

Flexibility on a two-teacher team is a condition that extends beyond scheduling. Students can move between two teachers individually, in small groups, or as a whole group. For example, imagine a school day in which one teacher is assisting students in conducting various experiments while in an adjacent room the other teacher helps students plan and write presentations. Students can easily move between one room and the other as they finish one part of a project or experiment and move onto another activity. They may even start an experiment, work on a presentation for a period of time, and then return to the experiment. With the guidance of the teacher, their time is planned by the logic of their activities rather than by inflexible blocks of time often still delineated by a bell.

The needs of teachers and students when practicing curriculum integration simply are better served by smaller teams. Consider the effort needed to plan curriculum with students and then imagine doing that planning several times a day with different groups of students. With a two-person team the fifty or so students can easily be pulled together as a single group. Further, various groups of students will require different resources; and although the teacher is not solely responsible for gathering those resources, he or she must still be cognizant of them. As previously emphasized, curriculum integration requires teachers to know their students very well, a condition that becomes more difficult with large numbers of students.

Special education schedules are also an instructional organization challenge for curriculum integration teachers. In many schools, students are pulled out of the classroom throughout the day, making it difficult to include all students for any substantial amount of time. Inclusion helps to meet these challenges with continual planning and mutual collaboration with the special education faculty and staff. As teachers become more skilled with curriculum integration, it becomes easier to meet individual needs within the regular classroom, thus decreasing the challenge of special education schedules.

In summary, although curriculum integration can be done in a variety of instructional organizations, given teachers who are dedicated to the philosophy, the best way to support curriculum integration is through small teams and flexible schedules. ⌘

18 What problems can develop with other faculty, and how can I deal with them?

When only one team practices curriculum integration, several problems with other teams and faculty are likely to occur. Some of these problems relate to honest questioning about the way students learn best and what should constitute the curriculum. Others are centered around doubts about personal teaching practices. With reservation of judgment, professional respect, and acceptance of differences, these potential difficulties can lead to rich conversations rather than dissension.

Curriculum integration represents a marked departure in philosophy from separate subject, teacher-driven curriculum. Teachers have honest differences about the best way to serve students, and new practices illuminate those differences. Curriculum integration teams initially may be placed on the defensive, having to explain their reasons for trying an unfamiliar practice. Although the teachers of curriculum integration may feel somewhat under fire, it is important that they patiently listen and respond to the concerns of their colleagues.

As with parents and administrators, other teachers also deserve the opportunity to learn about curriculum integration. Before or at the beginning of the school year, some presentations and discussions by the curriculum integration teachers may garner support or at least acceptance of the practice. Inviting students who have participated in curriculum integration to speak to teachers is a powerful activity. Former students can provide honest and valuable insights into both the challenges and triumphs of curriculum integration.

An example of sincere concern about the needs of young adolescents occurred in one school where an 8th grade team chose curriculum integration and the other 8th grade teams did not. Students would soon be sent to the high school, where teachers perceived practices to be very different from middle school. Teams who organized along separate subjects believed that students who participated in curriculum integration would have a difficult adjustment to high school. They wouldn't be accustomed to changing teachers and subjects every period or learning material not related to their own concerns. These separate subject specialist teachers were convinced that students wouldn't learn the content and skills needed to succeed in high school. The two curriculum integration teachers assured other teachers that they, too, were concerned about students' succeeding in high school and explained the reasons they believed curriculum integration would meet that goal. The whole group of 8th grade teachers then explored the meaning of "getting ready for high school." Did it mean that the 8th grade experience had to mock that of high school freshmen? Or was it at least as important to develop confident and involved learners? The discussion lasted all year and engendered much thought and mutual respect.

Honest and open communication between teams is critical. Discussion should focus on the outcomes of curriculum practices rather than the personalities of individual teachers or teams. It is important that the interaction be a discussion and not a lecture or admonition. Teachers make the decisions that they think are best for students based on their understandings and their perceived abilities. When some other choice seems to have additional benefits they have to question their own choice, whether publicly or privately. Questioning can lead to hostility or greater understanding, depending on the reaction to it. Neither preaching nor bragging is called for, but rather careful thought and professional discussion.

There may be, of course, a very few teachers who, while they recognize they could better serve their students, choose to take no action. They are unwilling to invest the time or thought required and avoid discussions about alternatives. To engage these teachers in discussion yields little except frustration. Efforts are better spent with other teachers.

Curriculum integration teachers, no matter how committed they are to the philosophy, do not have the right to judge the choices of other teachers. It is appropriate, however, to speak honestly about beliefs and practices and to be enthusiastic. It is also appropriate to mentor others who are interested in trying curriculum integration. Invitations for participation and resulting discussions unify teachers with diverse beliefs, while judgments about professional performance divide them.

Curriculum integration rests upon certain assumptions about young adolescents, the place of subject matter, and the role and relationships of students and teachers. These assumptions usually differ from those held by separate subject teachers. Practicing curriculum integration is likely to produce concern, questions, and sometimes contempt from others. Handled professionally, questions can lead to invigorating, reflective discussion and professional growth for all parties. When the concerns are ignored or degraded, the resulting division of teachers hurts the students being served. ⌘

Mark Springer, reflecting on his years directing the successful Watershed project offers these thoughts:

Can it happen? Despite daily vacillations, I remain optimistic. Looking at the big picture, I know change will come. There will always be individuals out there willing to fight or subvert the bureaucracy. True, there will always be doubters, reactionaries who hope somehow to push back the clock to some simpler time. There will always be the dreamless dead, but there will always be those as well who possess the creativity, sense of humor, and common sense to create a fresh program when the need exists but the system makes no provision for one. There will always be daring and resilient explorers willing to confront the frontiers of place, time, and quality and to push those boundaries further into the future.

Can it happen? It has to happen. One way or another, rivers always find their way to the sea.

19 What kind of personal and professional staff development is needed?

A warning issued long ago by Henry David Thoreau is particularly relevant as teachers and teams seek to implement curriculum integration. Thoreau advised: "Beware of enterprises that require new clothes, but not rather a new wearer of clothes." To succeed in this proposed curriculum adventure a teacher must, indeed, do more than put on the trappings and continue to teach essentially as before. Question #10 that describes the extensive changes in the role of teachers undertaking curriculum integration makes it obvious that considerable staff development will be necessary if the plan is to be successful.

The needed staff development or in-service programs have to be both long-term and interactive. Too often, teachers go to an inservice program to get new ideas and techniques. They seek ready-to-serve activities that promise to "motivate students." And while this approach is most understandable and not altogether inappropriate, curriculum integration will not be well served by attempting to rely on appealing activities or quick-fixes. Learning the tricks of the trade will not take the place of learning the trade itself.

Thoreau's warning cited above carries essentially the same principle as that stated decades ago by Alice Meil who summarized her extensive research on changing the curriculum with this valid maxim: "Changing the curriculum means changing people." And changing people is not done quickly or easily. Individuals need time to read and reflect. They need opportunities to dialogue with colleagues. And finally they need the encouragement to experiment, to make a start. Bringing in "visiting firemen" may be an effective way to stimulate discussion and set the stage, but no one-shot inservice program will suffice to initiate curriculum integration. Only as teachers' beliefs and commitments come to be compatible with the projected change and they possess a positive attitude will that new plant take root.

The ready availability of appropriate professional materials is essential. The annotated bibliography that comprises Question #20 provides a starting point. Copies of a number of these sources should be put in the hands of teachers, to take home and later to review in common planning time. The little book, *Student–Oriented Curriculum: Asking the Right Questions* [Alexander, 1996] is especially good for leading a team to instigate some changes. Members of a team cannot read and discuss this account of integrating the curriculum and come away without making a decision to move in this direction. The lessons these two teachers learned are powerful – and positive.

When faculty study groups are set up or when faculty meetings are focused on curriculum, discussions can lead to the idea of integrated learning. As they interact with colleagues, teachers are able to identify a teacher or two of like mind. Supporting one another this nucleus can take the initiative, request the opportunity to attend a conference, visit a school, and work with the administration to design next year's schedule so that they can experiment with curriculum integration.

As both stated and implied elsewhere in this document, implementing curriculum integration requires a supportive climate of collegiality, a belief in the potential of all kids, an expectation of professional growth and involvement, and the resources to make the needed changes operational. These conditions mandate staff development activities that are ongoing, localized, both informal and formal, that ensure interaction among and between faculty and staff, and otherwise support whatever it takes to change people. ⌘

> *Curriculum integration and motivation go hand in hand. Integrated curriculum provides experiences for students that are inherently compelling. Because students are engaged in meaningful learning stemming from their own interests and concerns, there is an intrinsic motivation to learn. Learning comes from within, from the desire to satisfy curiosities and know more about self and society. The process of learning then becomes as important as what is being learned.*
> — Pate, Homestead, & McGinnis in *Making Integrated Curriculum Work: Teachers, Students, and the Quest for Coherent Curriculum*, p. 8

20 Where can I secure more information?

F ortunately in the last decade a considerable body of professional literature dealing with curriculum integration has been amassed. There were excellent resources published in the 20s, 30s, and early 40s (most no longer available), but during the 50s, 60s, and 70s relatively few books were released that dealt specifically with any aspect of curriculum integration. In the sources cited below are a few of the early books that have continuing importance along with most of the relevant resources published in the 1990s.

A school or team considering curriculum integration would do well to amass a mini-library so teachers and others would be able to read and reflect on this major trend in curriculum. (The books cited below are available from National Middle School Association.)

Alexander, W., Carr, D., McAvoy, K. (1995). *Student-Oriented Curriculum: Asking the Right Questions.* The personal story of a school year in which two veteran teachers and their 40 sixth graders fully and successfully implemented a student-oriented curriculum. The lessons learned will encourage those who seek to empower students and integrate learning. (88 pages)

Beane, J. (1993). *A Middle School Curriculum: From Rhetoric to Reality.* A powerful book that has had and is continuing to have a major influence on the curriculum reform movement. A telling critique of the separate subject approach is followed by a proposal to establish a general education curriculum based on students' interests and societal needs. A must read for every serious middle level leader. (132 pages)

Beane, J. (1997). *Curriculum Integration: Designing the Core of Democratic Education*. Going well beyond other books on the subject, Beane details the history of curriculum integration and analyzes current critiques. Using classroom examples, *Curriculum Integration* provides a clear and insightful picture of the realities of democratic curriculum development and teaching. (122 pages)

Brazee, E., & Capelluti, J. (1995). *Dissolving Boundaries: Toward an Integrative Curriculum*. A solid rationale for implementing curriculum integration with a process for achieving it is followed by seven real stories of teams who have experimented with curriculum reform. Foreword by Beane. (160 pages)

Dickinson, T. (Ed.). (1993). *Readings in Middle School Curriculum: A Continuing Conversation*. The best thinking on middle school curriculum is brought together in this important volume. A few older articles are followed by an array of recent pieces written by such authors as Stevenson, Arnold, Erb, and Beane. (232 pages)

Dickinson, T., & Erb, T. (Eds.). (1996). *We Gain More Than We Give: Teaming in Middle Schools*. The most comprehensive book on middle level teaming ever published, this resource has extraordinary richness and depth. It provides new and valuable insights into the realities and nuances of teaming — its complexities, frustrations, benefits, and rewards. (568 pages)

Hawkins, M., & Graham, D. (1994). *Curriculum Architecture: Creating a Place of Our Own*. Refreshing, candid, and challenging, this publication's central message is that each school must create its own curriculum. Students, faculty, and community should all be actively involved in designing "a place of our own." (124 pages)

Lipka, R. Lounsbury, J., Toepfer, Jr., C., Vars, G., Allessi, Jr., S., & Kridel, C. (1998). *The Eight-Year Study Revisited: Lessons from the Past for the Present*. A reconsideration of the most extensive research study on curriculum ever conducted, this volume is one that all middle school and high schools need to study carefully. The findings of the Eight-Year Study, released in 1942 and never widely distributed, deserve our thoughtful attention — the lessons are particularly applicable today. (168 pages)

National Middle School Association. (1995). *This We Believe: Developmentálly Responsive Middle Level Schools.* Developed by a select committee and unanimously approved by NMSA's Board of Trustees, *This We Believe* provides clear guidance for those seeking to implement excellent educational programs for young adolescents. A strong rationale for middle level schools that summarizes what we know about young adolescents and the nature of our society, it includes a call for a curriculum that is challenging, integrative, and exploratory. (48 pages)

Pate, E., Homestead, E., & McGinnis, K. (1997). *Making Integrated Curriculum Work: Teachers, Students, and the Quest for Coherent Curriculum.* The story of a two-person, eighth grade team that — with the assistance of a college professor — established a democratic classroom for 58 students and embarked on a quest to discover a coherent curriculum. (161 pages)

Siu-Runyan, Y., & Faircloth, C.V. (Eds.). (1995). *Beyond Separate Subjects: Integrative Learning at the Middle Level.* A practical resource that will help teachers integrate the curriculum, this publication is organized into three sections — the whys and the whats, the specifics, and the building blocks. It contains honest descriptions from educators who have struggled to instigate change, as well as tips, ideas, and sample forms. (224 pages)

Springer, M. (1994). *Watershed: A Successful Voyage Into Integrative Learning.* The dream of a fully integrative curriculum is achievable — in an ordinary public school! Listen to the author as he chronicles the adventures of a two-person team in a full-day, experimental program that motivated 40 seventh graders to use real life activities and become responsible for their own learning. Inspirational and informative. (208 pages)

Stevenson, C., & Carr, J. (Eds.). (1993). *Integrated Studies in the Middle Grades: Dancing Through Walls.* These stories of successful experiences with a fully integrated curriculum written by the teachers who planned and conducted them will provoke imagination and nourish the courage to follow these "teachers of uncommon courage." (212 pages)

Vars, G. (1993). *Interdisciplinary Teaching in the Middle Grades: Why and How.* Begins with a rationale, overviews various organizational approaches and concerns, then provides practical guidance on planning, methods, and skill development. (88 pages)

Those interested in furthering their understanding of curriculum integration may want to consult the following references. These historically significant works should be available in most college and university libraries.

Dewey, J. (1956). *The Child and the Curriculum / The School and Society.* Chicago, IL: University of Chicago Press (Originally published in 1902 and 1900, respectively).

Dewey, J. (1938). *Experience and Education.* New York: Macmillan Publishing Company.

Faunce, R., and Bossing, N. (1951). *Developing the Core Curriculum.* New York: Prentic-Hall, Inc.

Hopkins, L. (1941). Interaction: *The Democratic Process.* New York: Heath.

Zapf, R. (1959). *Democratic Processes in the Secondary Classroom.* Englewood Cliffs, NJ: Prentice-Hall, Inc.

The periodical literature cited in Question 16 on page 43 should be recognized as important parts of the professional literature available on curriculum integration. ⌘

References

Aikin, W. M. (1942). *The story of the eight year study.* New York: Harper & Brothers.

Alexander, W. M., Carr, D., & McAvoy, K. (1995). *Student-oriented curriculum: Asking the right questions.* Columbus, OH: National Middle School Association.

American Educational Research Journal, 29 (2), 227-251.

Beane, J. A. (1993). *A middle school curriculum: From rhetoric to reality* (2nd ed.). Columbus, OH: National Middle School Association.

Beane, J. A. (1995). Curriculum integration and the disciplines of knowledge. *Phi Delta Kappan, 76* (8), 616-622.

Beane, J. A. (1997). *Curriculum integration: Designing the core of democratic education.* New York: Teachers College Press.

Beane, J. A. (1998). Reclaiming a democratic purpose for education. *Educational Leadership, 56* (2), 8-11.

Brandt, R. (Ed.). (1991). Integrating the curriculum. [Special Issue]. *Educational Leadership, 49* (2).

Brandt, R. (Ed.). (1995) Self-renewing schools [Special Issue]. *Educational Leadership, 52* (7).

Brazee, E. N., & Capelluti, J. (1995). *Dissolving boundaries: Toward an integrative curriculum.* Columbus, OH: National Middle School Association.

Dewey, J. (1938). *Experience and education.* New York: Macmillan Publishing Company.

Dewey, J. (1956). *The child and the curriculum/The school and society.* Chicago, IL: University of Chicago Press. (Originally published in 1902 and 1900, respectively.)

Dickinson, T. (Ed.). (1993). *Readings in middle school curriculum: A continuing conversation.* Columbus, OH: National Middle School Association.

Erb, T. (Ed.). (1996). Curriculum integration: Proceeding with cautious optimism [Special Issue]. *Middle School Journal, 28* (1).

Erb, T. (Ed.). (1998a). Curricular coherence: The conversation continues [Special Issue]. *Middle School Journal, 29* (4).

Erb, T. (Ed.). (1998b). Curriculum reform: Disciplinary, interdisciplinary, & integrated [Special Issue]. *Middle School Journal, 30* (2).

Faunce, R. C.., & Bossing, N. L. (1951). *Developing the core curriculum.* New York: Prentice-Hall, Inc.

Hopkins, L. T. (Ed.). (1937). *Integration: Its meaning and application.* New York: D. Appleton-Century Company.

Lipka, R. P., Lounsbury, J. H., Toepfer, C. F., Jr., Vars, G. F., Alessi, S. P., Jr., & Kridel, C. (1998). *The eight-year study revisited: Lessons from the past for the present.* Columbus, OH: National Middle School Association.

National Middle School Association (1995). *This we believe: Developmentally responsive middle level schools.* Columbus, OH: Author.

Pate, P. E., Homestead, E. R., & McGinnis, K. L. (1997). *Making integrated curriculum work: Teachers, students, and the quest for coherent curriculum.* New York: Teachers College Press.

Springer, M. (1994). *Watershed: A successful voyage into integrative learning.* Columbus, OH: National Middle School Association

Vars, G. (1993). *Interdisciplinary teaching in the middle grades: Why and How.* Columbus, OH: National Middle School Association

Vars, G. (1997). Student concerns and standards too. *Middle School Journal, 28* (4), pp. 44-49.

Zapf, R. M. (1959). *Democratic processes in the secondary classroom.* Englewood Cliffs, NJ: Prentice-Hall, Inc.

APPENDIX

A Planning Process for Achieving Curriculum Integration

James Beane has been a strong advocate of student involvement, democratic practices, and a truly integrated curriculum. Below are outlined the steps he and Barbara Brodhagen have used in implementing the type of curriculum described in his books. While it has sometimes been seen simply as a way to increase student interest and engagement, it is actually intended to create a particular kind of curriculum with student participation. They report that this process works well with various groups and age levels.

1. Students are asked to do some self-reflection, think about themselves.
   Who are you?
   What are you like?
   What are your interests or aspirations?

   Then they are asked to compile a list of words or phrases that they would use if asked to tell about themselves.

2. The first of two major questions is then asked.
   Still thinking about yourself and looking at the lists you have made, what are the questions or concerns you have about yourself?
   List them.

3. After sufficient time for individuals to make their lists, form small groups of five or six people and ask them to search for shared or common questions. (No one is required to show his/her personal lists or share anything unless he/she cares to do so.) As common concerns are identified list them on newsprint.

4. After the group's self-questions and concerns are recorded, turn to the second major question.
   Now we would like you to look outside yourself at the world you live in, from the parts closest — family, friends, community — to the more distant parts — state, nation, the world. Think about that world, both near and far, and list questions or concerns you have about the world. What questions do you have about the world you live in?

5. After individuals have had time to individually record questions or concerns, they are again placed in small groups and asked to identify and list shared "world" questions and concerns.

6. While still in small groups ask them to look at the lists of self and world questions and identify possible themes for the curriculum.

   Are there cases where there are connections between self and world questions such as conflict in school and conflict in the larger world? *If so, what are some words or phrases that we might use to name the connections, such as 'conflict?'*

   (In a single class or relatively small group this step may be undertaken by the total class reviewing the posted lists from the groups.)

7. The lists of themes are then posted where everyone can see them, and the large group reaches consensus on a single list. A vote is taken to determine the first theme for study.

8. Groups are reconvened to identify questions from their lists that might be included under the theme selected.
   What are specific self and world questions and concerns we might want to answer within this theme? Be sure to indicate which questions are of interest to all or most of your group and which ones to one or two, since there will be room for both large and small group activities.

   (A steering committee comprised of representatives from each group helps organize this work.)

9. Finally, ask students to identify possible activities the group might engage in and resources they might use in seeking answers to the questions. This activity could be done with small groups, the whole class, or a combination.

10. Teachers then organize and expand the activities, develop a tentative calendar, assign groups, and otherwise set the stage for student research, discussion, and sharing.

About the Authors

Gert Nesin is currently completing a doctoral program at the University of Georgia in Athens. She has been an elementary teacher, a middle school team teacher, and an assistant principal in Maine and North Carolina. She was nominated as Maine's Teacher of the Year in 1992 and recently garnered the Outstanding Teaching Assistant Award at the University of Georgia. Active professionally, Gert has presented at many state, regional, and national conferences and institutes.

John Lounsbury, Publications Editor for the National Middle School Association, has been involved in middle level education for several decades, particularly as a writer, speaker, and consultant. Dean Emeritus of the School of Education, Georgia College & State University, Milledgeville, he is recognized as a key leader in the movement and as a strong advocate for young adolescents.